3.3/2012
7.8/2015

First published in Great Britain in 2008 by Quercus

Quercus
21 Bloomsbury Square
London
WC1A 2NS

Text and illustations © Peter Kent, 2008

A CIP catalogue reference for this book is available
from the British Library

ISBN 978 1 84724 433 8

10 9 8 7 6 5 4 3 2 1

Printed and bound in China

TAKE A

FLIGHT

PETER KENT

How to Use this Book

Take a Flight can be used either at home or taken as a companion on a journey. This book is packed with fantastically detailed illustrations that will entertain and engage your child. To make the most of this book, encourage your child to describe what they can see and ask questions about the pictures.

Interactive fun!
There are two types of activities in the book:

 This symbol indicates an activity to be done using the illustrations in the book.

 This indicates an activity to be done during an actual flight.

Where are they?
Three fun images have been hidden throughout the book. How many times can your child spot the pink scooter, the teddy bear and the seagull?

We hope you and your child have
fun using this book!

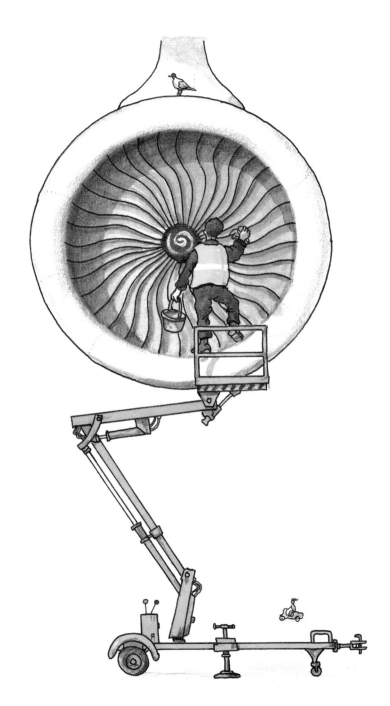

Contents

The Airport

This is an airport from high above. It has:

→ A **runway** where planes can take off and land
→ A **terminal** where you can check in your bags and wait for your plane
→ A **fire station** with fire engines
→ A **control tower** where the planes are watched and told what to do
→ A **car park** for passengers and airport staff

Count how many planes you see parked at the airport.

Find out the name of the airport you are flying from.

runway

30

8

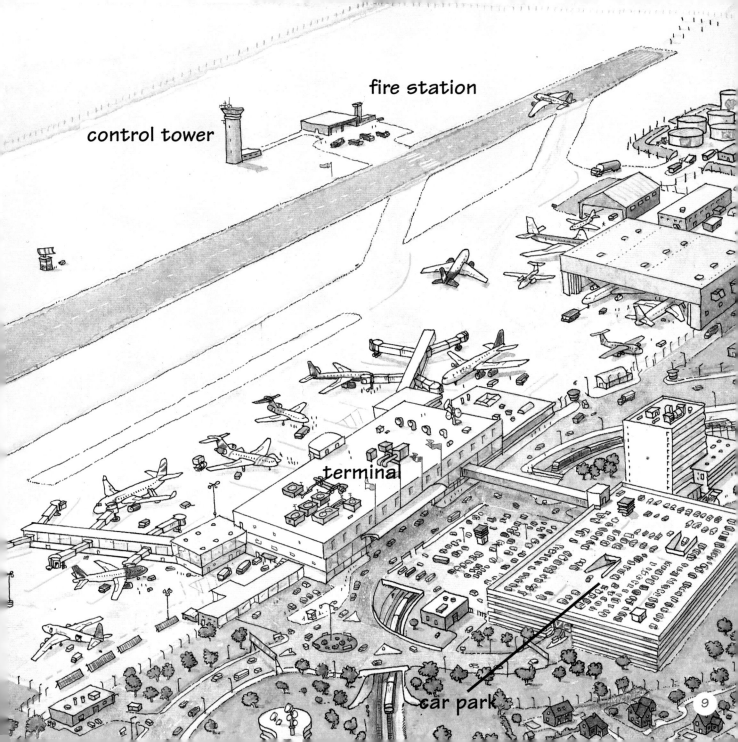

control tower

fire station

terminal

car park

9

Check in

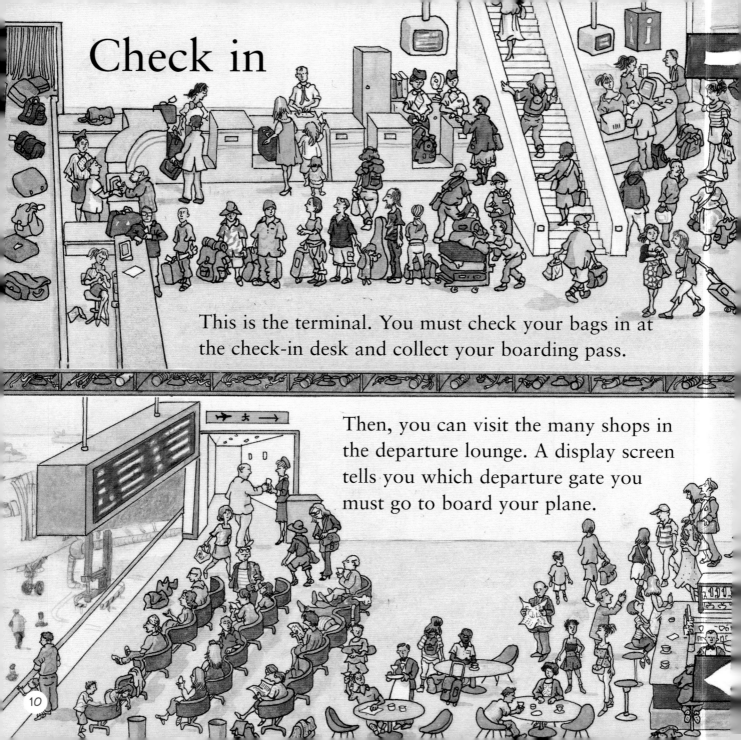

This is the terminal. You must check your bags in at the check-in desk and collect your boarding pass.

Then, you can visit the many shops in the departure lounge. A display screen tells you which departure gate you must go to board your plane.

You will then go through security control where they check your passport and your hand luggage.

Look at the pictures carefully. Explain what you see happening.

The **tail fin** (helps the plane turn right and left)

On the Ground

Here is a plane at an airport. In a day it will fly four times from London to Paris and back.

When it is flying, it has seven flight crew. When it is on the ground, lots of people help to get the plane ready for the next flight. They are called the **ground crew.**

The plane **wings**

How many ground crew
can you see in the picture?
What are they doing?

At the airport can you see
any planes that are being
prepared on the ground?

The plane **nose**

13

Machines at the Airport

Some machines at the airport are very low so they can pass underneath the planes. Some can stretch themselves like a crane to reach up to the planes. The machines usually have warning lights and stripes to make them easy to see.

Transporter – this carries all kinds of things to and from the plane.

Electric buggy – this is used to carry elderly or ill passengers around the airport.

Tugs – these are very strong and are used to pull planes! They come in different sizes.

Tractors – this small tractor is useful for pulling luggage trolleys and other equipment.

Luggage trolley – this takes your luggage to and from the plane.

Can you remember the name of each machine?

How many of these machines can you see at the airport?

Mobile staircase –
this staircase is driven to
the plane to allow you to
climb up to the plane door.

Luggage elevator – this takes
your bags from the luggage
trolleys into the plane.

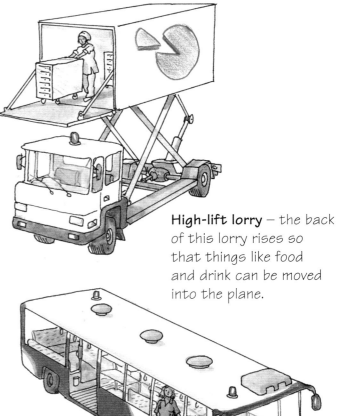

High-lift lorry – the back
of this lorry rises so
that things like food
and drink can be moved
into the plane.

Passenger bus – this bus
carries you from the terminal
to the plane.

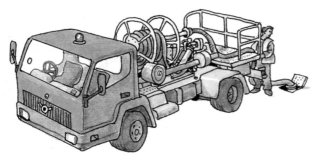

Fuel bowser – this fills up the plane's fuel tank.

15

Cargo Hold and Cockpit

A plane carries a lot of packages as well as people and luggage. The packages and luggage are kept in the **cargo hold** underneath where the passengers sit.

cargo hold

Pilots sit in the **cockpit** which is full of computers that help them fly the plane. There are always two pilots on a plane.

 Look at the ground crew in this picture. What is each person doing?

 As you are boarding the plane can you see the cargo holds?

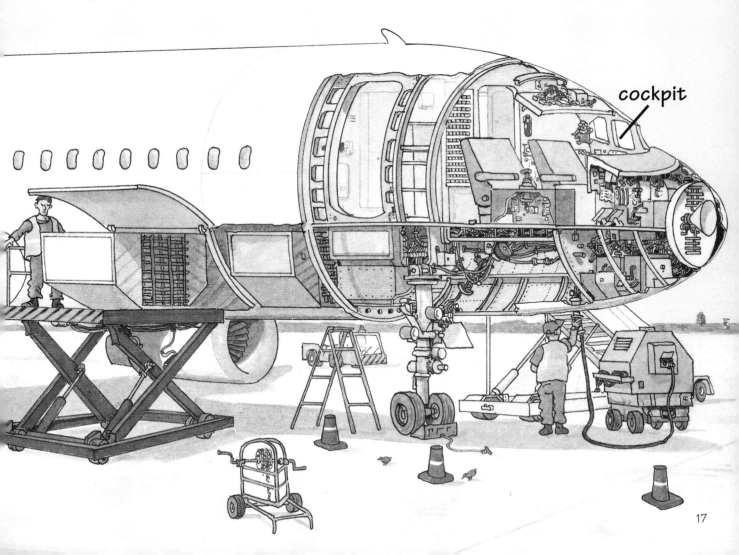

cockpit

Engines and Fuel

A plane usually has two **engines**. The engines are powerful and this helps the plane fly fast. Planes keep fuel in their wings. Before it flies, a plane must be filled up with fuel!

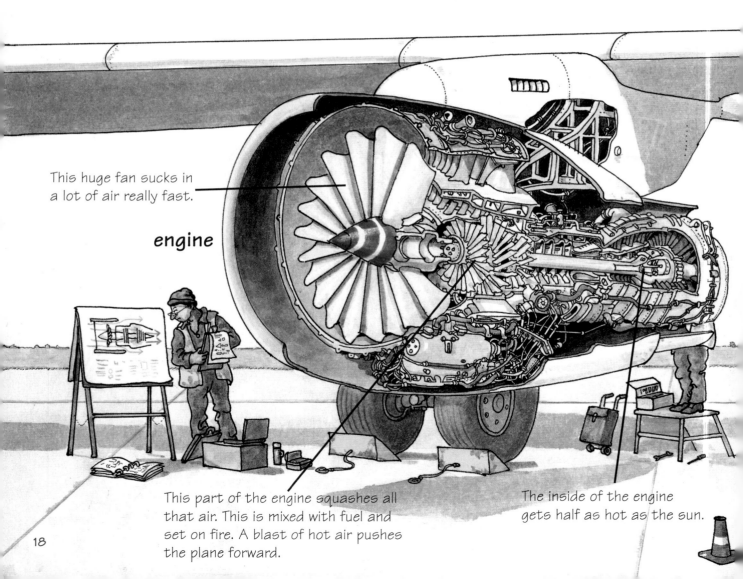

This huge fan sucks in a lot of air really fast.

engine

This part of the engine squashes all that air. This is mixed with fuel and set on fire. A blast of hot air pushes the plane forward.

The inside of the engine gets half as hot as the sun.

What is the name of the machine filling up the wings?

Can you see any planes with four engines?

19

Stocking Up

When a plane lands and the passengers get off, the ground crew bring more food and drinks and anything else needed.

When you flush a toilet on a plane, everything in the toilet is sucked to a tank at the back of the plane. Every time the plane lands the tank is emptied into a **lavatory lorry**.

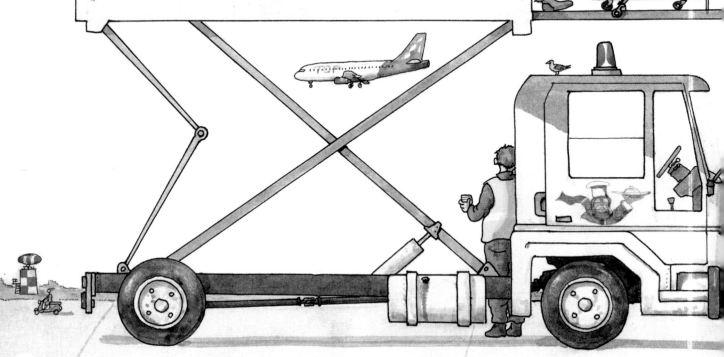

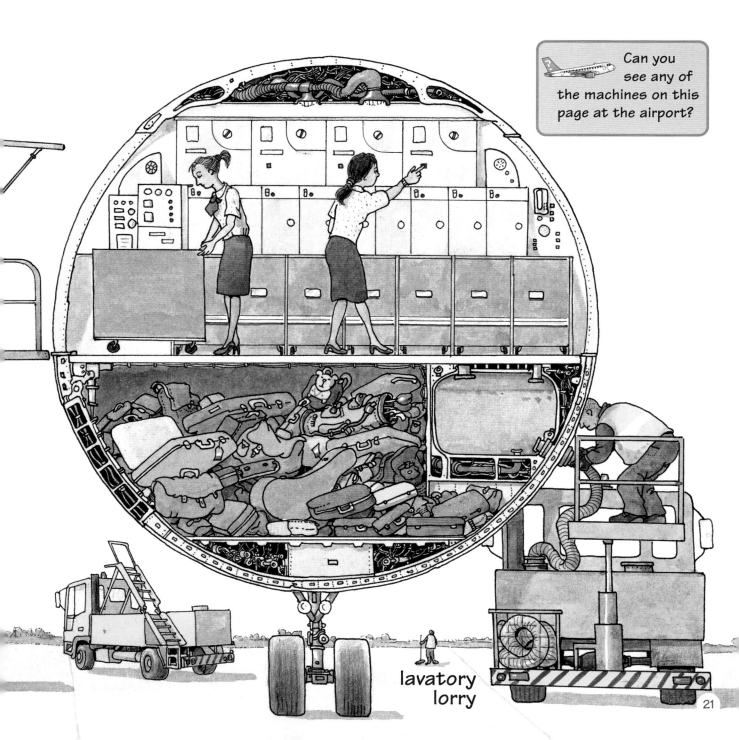

Can you see any of the machines on this page at the airport?

lavatory lorry

Check List

Before the plane takes off, the pilots walk around the plane checking that it is ready to fly. In the cockpit, they check all the **switches** and **dials** as well. When the checks are finished, the plane is ready to fly.

Safety Demonstration

During a safety demonstration, the cabin crew point out where the emergency exits are. They also show you how to put on a life jacket and an oxygen mask.

Taking Off

Now it is time to take off! Each plane has to wait in turn to use the runway. When the runway is clear, the pilot drives the plane to the runway, speeds down really fast and then takes off into the air.

Wings

Take off

If you look outside your window, you will see the wings of the plane. These are what help the plane fly. When a plane is about to take off you can hear and see the wings becoming bigger.

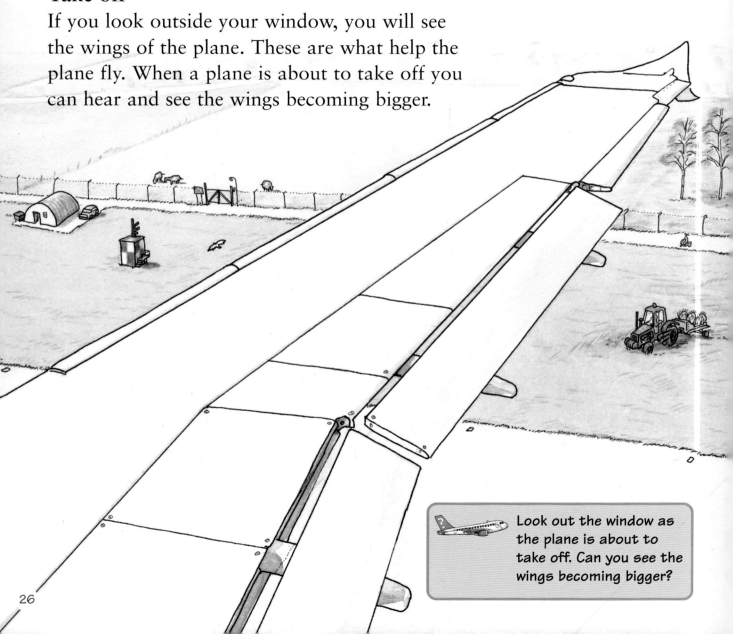

Look out the window as the plane is about to take off. Can you see the wings becoming bigger?

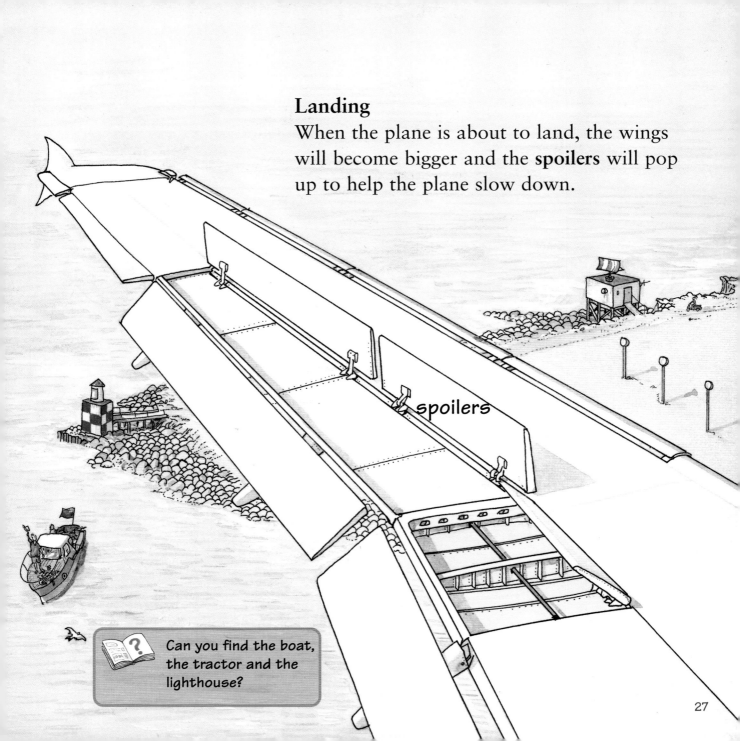

Landing

When the plane is about to land, the wings will become bigger and the **spoilers** will pop up to help the plane slow down.

spoilers

Can you find the boat, the tractor and the lighthouse?

Meal Time

Once you are in the air, you will be offered food and drinks. This food has been made in a kitchen and has been brought to the plane in a catering truck. This is then warmed up in the galley on the plane. The pilots must each eat a different meal, so that if one meal is bad only one

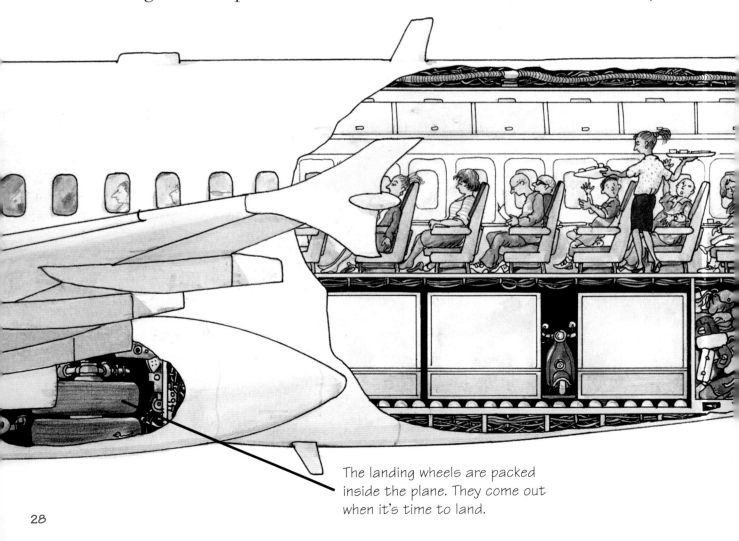

The landing wheels are packed inside the plane. They come out when it's time to land.

pilot will be sick. Sometimes they bring their own sandwiches!

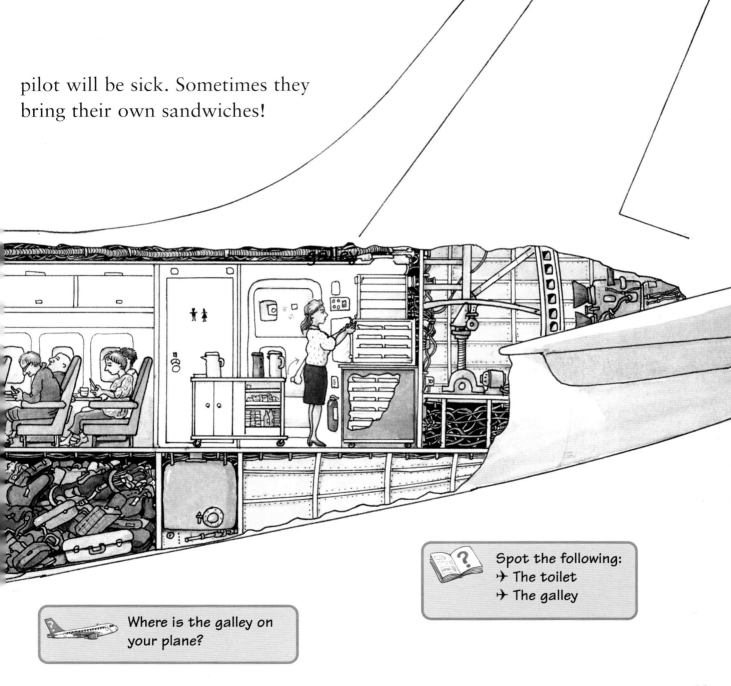

Where is the galley on your plane?

Spot the following:
✈ The toilet
✈ The galley

At Your Seat

Look around you when are sitting in your plane seat. You will see a small **TV** screen where you can watch movies, a **seat pocket** where you will find **headphones** for the TV, magazines and a safety leaflet. You will have a **tray** in front of you for your meal. You can pull down the **window shutter** if you want to go to sleep!

window shutter

TV

tray

headphones

seat pocket

On the seat arm you have a remote control for the TV, a button to turn on your own light and a button to call the flight crew. **Seat belts** are really important. You should wear one during take off and landing and throughout the flight, especially when the seat belt sign is on.

Can you see the seat belt sign on your plane?

seat belt

Landing

Lots of planes fly in the sky. The sky can get crowded and have traffic jams.

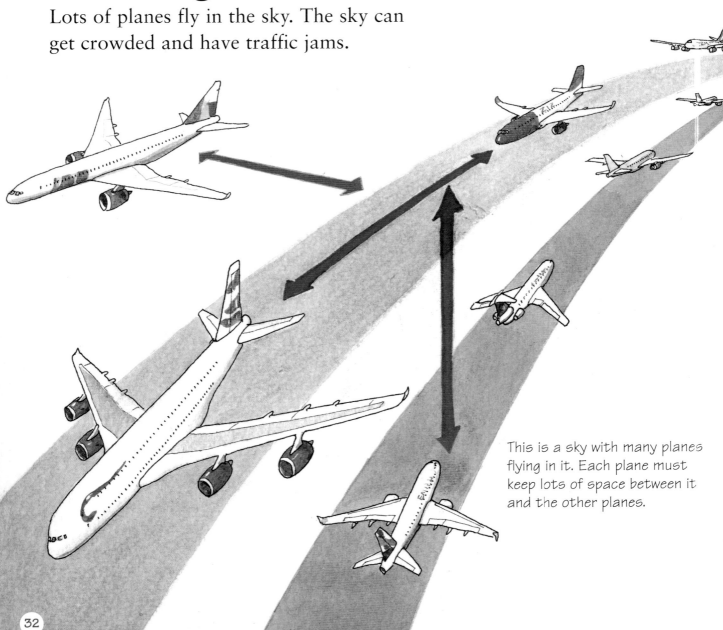

This is a sky with many planes flying in it. Each plane must keep lots of space between it and the other planes.

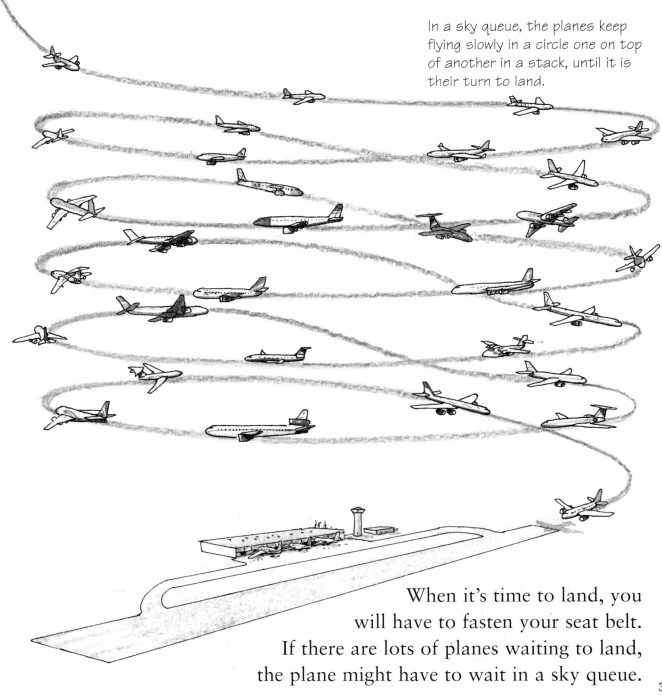

In a sky queue, the planes keep flying slowly in a circle one on top of another in a stack, until it is their turn to land.

When it's time to land, you will have to fasten your seat belt. If there are lots of planes waiting to land, the plane might have to wait in a sky queue.

Leaving the Plane

When the plane lands it parks by the terminal. A mobile staircase will be driven to the door so that the passengers can leave the plane.

While the passengers are getting off, the luggage trolleys arrive. They will take your luggage to the terminal for you to collect.

At some airports, a passenger bus will come and collect you from the plane. It will take you to the terminal, where you can pick up your bags.

Count the number of passengers leaving the plane. How many children can you see?

As you leave the plane, make sure you say goodbye to the flight crew!

Leaving the Airport

At **passport control**, you will wait in a queue and hand over your passport to be stamped.

Then you walk to the luggage collection. Here you will find the moving **carousel**, where you will collect your bags.

On the carousel, can you see any bags with ribbons or labels? Why do you think people add these to their bags?

Once you have passed through **customs** you can leave the airport. Your journey is now complete!

How many blue bags can you see on the carousel?

37